Grandma's Wrinkles

Written By Glenda Sisk

One sunny, Saturday morning I was sitting in the kitchen, eating my favorite breakfast of pancakes. Out of nowhere, mama announced we were going to go visit Great Grandma Annie today! My older brother, Matt, wasn't very happy to hear this. He groaned and complained that he was going to miss the big baseball game if he went. Mama crossed her arms, held up her chin and replied "Matthew James, you should honor every day you see you're grandma. Everyone will go today, you and your sister Jessica, so go get ready now!" I giggled and took a forkful of blueberry pancakes. I didn't mind at all, I loved going to see my Great Grandma Annie. I looked forward to climbing up in her lap and rocking with her. She'd tell me the grandest stories about her life, too! Great Grandma Annie likes to call me Jessie Jo. She has lots of wrinkles! I asked mama "Why does Great Grandma Annie have so many wrinkles?" My mama smiled and said, "It's because she is 99 years old, but why don't you ask her yourself? Now go get ready little girl before I leave you here!" Mama said with a smile. I think it's because she smiles so much her face just kind of got stuck like that!

As we rode to Great Grandma Annie's home, I wondered what story she would tell me today. I closed my eyes; and I could see Great Grandma Annie sitting in her chair, rocking and humming. I'd burst into the room and climb into her outstretched arms and she would give me the biggest and best hug I'd ever get. I'd smell the apple pie baked on her clothes and ask for a story. She'd smile at me and start about somewhere far away and old. I try to remember back to my favorite story, but I just keep getting side tracked with others. Once she told about a time when her whole family rode in a horse and wagon from Arkansas to Kentucky! What a great adventure that was! I tried to imagine all her brothers and sisters crammed in the wagon. She said it took days to get there and they got to camp out when it got dark and sleep in the wagon.

Another time she told me a story about living on the farm with a bunch of animals. She would get up before the sun was up and milk cows, feed the chickens and pigs, and then she would help her mama with cooking lunch and dinner. She would laugh and tell me how she'd escape from the kitchen and chase the chickens around the barnyard, then she would sigh and shake her head, her eyes far away as she said her life had been hard but, filled with a lot of love and laughter as well.

Her favorite story was the one when she met Great Grandpa Bud. She went to a party in town and saw Great Grandpa Bud from across the room. She thought he was the most handsome young man she had ever seen in her life. After a few minutes of giggling and waving shyly at him, Great Grandpa Bud summoned up enough courage and asked Great Grandma Annie out for a date. He was so nervous that he took a drink with the dipper out of the dish pan instead of the water bucket and spit suds all over the floor. Great Grandma Annie thought that was so funny, she knew he was the man for her when he laughed at himself too; she just had to say yes. Great Grandpa Bud has been dead for 25 years now, but not a day goes by that she doesn't miss him. My mama said you can see it in her eyes. Great Grandma Annie would always smile softly and say she had a wonderful life with him.

She said once, that one of her saddest days was when my Uncle Harry died. It was July 17th 1944. He was her first born son and went off to fight in World War II and he never came back. She said he looked so handsome in his uniform! Her heart swelled with pride as he went off to defend our country. She said World War II was a terrible time for our country and boys fighting that war. Many families lost sons, fathers, brothers, and husbands in that war. She said freedom sometimes requires a high price. She said she never gave up hope that he was still alive until they sent his hero's body home to her. She always said she was proud of him for fighting for our freedom, but he was still just her little boy and it left a great big hole in her heart that still there today. Sometimes she would pull out his letters and read them to me. She would even let me hold the Medal of Honor they sent back home with him. This story always made her sad and you could always see a tear escape when she told it.

Then she'd always have to talk about something much happier. She'd laugh endlessly at all the fun she'd had with her mischievous boys. Those boys used to go swimming down at the pond on the way home from school and they would come home all soggy wet and dripping all over her clean floors. One day, Great Grandma Annie was tired of all those dirty clothes, and was afraid something might happen to them. So, from that day she'd punish them for swimming down at the pond! But the boys tried to outsmart her, deciding they should take off their clothes before swimming to appear being dry when they got home. When Great Grandma Annie found out about this, she got smarter! She'd sew a piece of thread on each of her son's buttons, so they couldn't take them off without her knowing! She'd laugh out loud and finally say she got those boys to behave!

My great Grandma Annie is so wise. I remember asking her one time what she thought Heaven was like. She smiled at me and her eyes said a thousand words. She said she thought Heaven was like finally going home after a long journey. Her heart was there with all the family that was waiting on her. She said she didn't want anyone to cry sorrowful tears for her. She held her head high and said she wanted tears of joy for her passing. And of course I wanted to know why. She said it was because she would be reunited with all her loved ones, Great Grandpa Bud, Uncle Harry. She said when my time came to come to Heaven to not be scared because she would be waiting for me with open arms.

Finally we're here! I jumped out of the car and bounded straight up the steps and through the door. It only took me moments to find Great Grandma Annie, "Why do you have so many wrinkles?" I blurted out cutting her hello short. She smiled her ageless smile, kissed my cheek and gathered me into her lap. "Nice to see you too, darling" She replied with twinkling eyes. She then touched her own face almost self-consciously, that unsure moment passing into happiness.

I see my life reflected back at me in a thousand laughs, smiles, tears, words, and love all inside my skin. All my wisdom is too there to be seen in my face and body. I'm 99 years old and I have a wrinkle for every smile I've shared, every person I've loved and every year I've lived and I have lived a long time and loved a lot of people including your mama, brother and you. I couldn't ask for a better look than my own. I laugh and think over her words for a moment then ask for a story. She hugs me tighter and laughs and begins to go on about a garden she used to tend. I look at her face as her lips move, and then her hands that cradle me softly, then the feet that rock us and I smile thinking that when I grow up I too hope I'm lucky enough to have as many wrinkles as my Great Grandma Annie.

Vabella Publishing
P.O. Box 1052
Carrollton, Georgia 30112
www.vabella.com

©Copyright 2017 by Glenda Sisk

All rights reserved. No part of the book may be reproduced or utilized in any form or by any means without permission in writing from the author. All requests should be addressed to the publisher.

13-digit ISBN 978-1-942766-46-9

10 9 8 7 6 5 4 3 2 1

www.ingramcontent.com/pod-product-compliance
Lightning Source LLC
Chambersburg PA
CBHW041507220426
43661CB00017B/1270